"*The Anxiety Workbook for Kids* is very child-friendly and engaging. It offers children and adolescents concrete and effective strategies for calming their fears and taking control of their lives. The workbook provides helpful techniques for children to become the bosses of their imagination so it serves them well. Children who use this workbook will undoubtedly master their worries, feel more positive about themselves and their lives, and interact more confidently with others. *The Anxiety Workbook for Kids* is a must-have for any therapist or counselor working with children, and for any family concerned about a child with anxiety."

—**Nadine J. Kaslow, PhD, ABPP**, Emory University; 2014 president of the American Psychological Association

"With inventive illustrations and activities, Alter and Clarke excel at explaining worry and cognitive-behavioral strategies to young readers. Whether a child's worries are improbable or impossible, readers will benefit from these practical tools which engage the strength of imagination. A great resource for kids as well as parents and teachers."

—**Andrea Umbach, PsyD**, clinical psychologist and author of *Conquer Your Fears and Phobias for Teens*

"*The Anxiety Workbook for Kids* provides families with a wonderful tool for helping the growing number of children experiencing problems of anxiety: the child's own imagination. Robin Alter and Crystal Clarke have created a much-needed resource that is not just thoroughly engaging, but extremely beneficial."

—**Stuart Shanker**, distinguished research professor of philosophy and psychology at York University

The Anxiety Workbook for Kids

Take Charge of Fears & Worries
Using the Gift of Imagination

ROBIN ALTER, PhD
CRYSTAL CLARKE, MSW

ILUSTRATIONS BY OLIVER BURNS

Instant Help Books
An Imprint of New Harbinger Publications, Inc.

Publisher's Note

This publication is designed to provide accurate and authoritative information in regard to the subject matter covered. It is sold with the understanding that the publisher is not engaged in rendering psychological, financial, legal, or other professional services. If expert assistance or counseling is needed, the services of a competent professional should be sought.

Distributed in Canada by Raincoast Books

Cover design by Amy Shoup

Cover photo is a model used for illustrative purposes only.

Acquired by Tesilya Hanauer

Library of Congress Cataloging-in-Publication Data

18   17   16

10   9   8   7   6   5   4   3   2   1   First Printing

Dedications

I would like to dedicate this book to all of the children that my coauthor, Dr. Robin Alter, and I have been fortunate to work with, and learn from, throughout the years. From you, we've learned so much about how worries can get in the way of kids fully enjoying life, and about the creative ways that kids can take charge of their worries so they can build their confidence and enjoy more of what life has to offer. Without all of you, this book would not have been possible. I feel privileged to have been able to work with so many of you in this way, and I am constantly amazed by the strength, creativity, and imagination inside each and every one of you.

I would also like to express my gratitude to Dr. Robin Alter for adding fuel to my interest in helping children to empower themselves by partnering with that strong, creative force within themselves, rather than experiencing it as working against them. And for being my partner throughout our own creative journey of preparing this book in the hope that it may reach, and be of help to, many more children in the future.

Crystal Clarke, MSW, RSW

I want to thank all the children who were so generous and eager to share their imaginations with me, and the parents who were willing to give a new approach a solid try. All of you helped me to see the connection between anxiety and imagination, which led to my first book, *Anxiety and the Gift of Imagination,* and eventually to this workbook.

I want to thank my coauthor, Crystal Clarke, for her dedication and thoroughness in this project. She was on board with the imagination/ anxiety connection even before we began our collaboration. Crystal's keen understanding of how children think and what will capture their interest and imaginations was integral to the quality of this workbook.

And to Dr. Christine Littlefield, my friend and colleague, who urged me to write a workbook and wouldn't let up until I did. Without you this book would never have happened. Thank you for that, and for so much more. You live on.

Robin Alter, PhD

We would both like to thank our illustrator, Oliver Burns, for his attention to our vision. Oliver precisely captured each emotion and message that we wanted to convey, while maintaining the simplicity that we felt was important in aiming to create a comfortable space for children as they are invited to add their own art to the workbook. Thank you, Oliver, for lending us your incredible imagination in bringing our imaginations, and our workbook, to life!

Crystal Clarke and Robin Alter

The Anxiety Workbook for Kids

Contents

The Anxiety Workbook for Kids

A Letter to Parents

We understand the concern and frustration that can come with wishing you could help your child manage anxiety and enjoy all that life has to offer. We've worked with hundreds of children, and have heard from as many parents about how difficult it can be for a parent to see a child incapacitated by fear and worry. Whether your child is unable to sleep, focus, get to school, or engage in experiences they might otherwise enjoy, we know your heart goes out to them. We want to give you and your child tools that can help you both when anxiety gets in the way.

The Anxiety Workbook for Kids is truly a workbook like no other. This book creates opportunities for kids to get to know their anxiety, and where it comes from, by engaging in fun activities that foster positivity. These activities will help children understand the roles that the mind and imagination play in anxiety. Because children usually view imagination as a positive trait and something that they can be proud of, they're often more open to interventions that use an imaginative and playful approach. When children are empowered by the idea that they can take control of their mind and imagination, they tend to show increased confidence, optimism, and strength when trying to understand and manage their anxiety.

This workbook begins by providing answers to the questions typically asked by children about anxiety, but in fun, engaging, and nonthreatening ways. It then moves on to helping children learn more about their own anxiety through art, activities, and games. Learning about anxiety in this way is important for kids—to manage anxiety, they first need to know how it impacts them, then how to recognize it, and finally how to deal with their anxiety using the strengths they already have!

This book includes a focus on skills and strategies that are known to be helpful for kids when dealing with anxiety: positive thinking, problem solving, communication and assertiveness, gradual exposure steps, and relaxation and mindfulness activities. However, what makes this book truly unique is that it also focuses on an area that's often neglected: the **imagination**. Children's anxieties sometimes have to do with real situations or events, but much of the time, their anxieties are related to things that are either impossible or extremely unlikely. In effect, children can become anxious about things they imagine are happening. This book will help children understand the role their imagination plays in relation to their anxiety. It will help them become the master of their own imagination by directing it where they want it to go. This approach has proven to be an empowering resource for children, and we hope that this workbook will help your child learn to manage anxiety by using the powerful gifts of the mind and the imagination. By doing this, your child will be able to more comfortably and wholeheartedly enjoy life to the fullest!

If you feel like this sometimes, turn the page. This book can help!

Chapter 1

Questions and Answers

What Is Anxiety?

You may be wondering (lots of people do)…
what is **anxiety**? Is it the same as a **worry**? What
about **fear**? Are these things the same or are they
different?

Let's think about these words for a minute…

Fear is the feeling we get when our body and brain tell us that we could be in
some kind of danger. This is how humans stay safe—fear tells us to protect
ourselves. But sometimes fear can also stop us from doing things we might enjoy.

**This book will help you learn
some ways to deal with fear!**

Worry can feel like a type of fear that sticks around in our mind. Maybe it comes
around a lot, especially in certain situations. We might worry about scary things
we think *could* happen. We might worry about things that probably won't happen
at all. We might even worry about things that we know aren't real or possible (like
monsters under the bed). Even though we know some things aren't real, our
worries can still feel very real!

**Our imagination can be a lot of fun sometimes, but
it can also get us to imagine lots of things to worry
about. Keep reading…this book can help you practice
ways to be the boss of your own imagination!**

Anxiety is what we feel in our mind and our body when our worries hang around a lot. A thought about something bad that could happen might get stuck in our head and it might be hard to stop thinking about it. Our face might start to feel hot and sweaty, or it might feel like there is a big lump in our stomach. We might think that this is just the type of person we are. Sometimes we might feel anxious but not know why. At other times, we might have a reason to be anxious, but our reaction is too strong for the situation, and it gets in the way of us enjoying life. And sometimes, we imagine a reason to feel anxious—and it can feel very real!

**Fear, anxiety, and worry are similar, so it's easy to see
how people often talk about them in the same way.
You can use the words that feel right for you.**

Why Do We Worry?

Have you ever wondered why we worry, or even panic, about some things that other people might say are "nothing to worry about"? Why do our mind and body tell us to worry?

Our brain and our body are pretty smart. We're born with certain **responses** or **reactions** that help keep us safe.

One example is hunger. It tells us that our body needs food for energy. We need to eat to be healthy and keep living! But sometimes we feel

like eating even when our body isn't really hungry. Maybe the food just looks really good and we know we'll enjoy it, or maybe we're just eating because we're bored. The basic hunger response works, but it's not perfect.

Our **response to danger** is also pretty good, but it's not perfect. Sometimes the things we fear might not be dangerous at all—we may imagine that a thing is much more dangerous than it really is.

For example, some kids worry about getting a shot because they think it will be really painful. But most of us know that needles only hurt a little, and shots can help us a lot. Another example is clowns— some kids have a fear of clowns, even though they aren't a threat at all. Can you think of any other examples of things we worry about that aren't really dangerous?

How We Deal with Danger: Fight, Flight, Freeze, and Beyond

Our mind and body have some smart ways to DEAL WITH DANGER! These are called the **3 Fs**:

1. **Fight**: stay and defend, or stand up for, ourselves

2. **Flight**: get away from (or **flee**) the danger quickly

3. **Freeze**: stay still and do nothing while our mind goes blank

The **3 Fs** are our body's natural response to danger, but people have some other reactions when they are feeling scared and worried too! Turn the page to learn about them.

In addition to the **3 Fs**, there are two more ways people sometimes react when they feel scared or worried:

1. **Be around people** who help us feel safe and comfortable.

   Who do I feel safe around?

   Can I do this on my own yet, or is there someone who could help or encourage me?

Or, with practice, we can even:

2. Find a way to **relax**, stay present, and think about the problem. Ask yourself:

   Am I really in danger?

   What are my choices?

   If I defend myself, could I win?

   Or could it make things worse?

   What would make me feel safe and calm?

   Who, or what, might help?

   What steps should I take?

So we've learned that we have some fear and anxiety for really important reasons: they can help **protect us** and **keep us safe**. If something threatens us, it's important that we feel fear so we can either get away from the danger or defend ourselves.

But it's also important to be able to tell when we're in real danger, or if our imagination has only made the danger seem real (or at least bigger than it really is). This will help our brain and body choose the most helpful reaction.

This next story will help you understand more about why we sometimes have such a big reaction to things that we only *imagine* are dangerous.

Many, many years ago, life for humans was very different. People didn't live in houses with burglar alarms. We lived close to wild animals. Sometimes we even lived close to tribes of other humans who weren't always friendly. Life for everybody wasn't as safe as it is now. We lived with real danger in our lives every day, so we had to be alert all the time. We had a lot of practice with the fight, flight, and freeze responses. When humans do things over and over for millions of years, our brain and body remember those behaviors. Those behaviors become a part of us. Isn't that cool?

So, let's think about how it might have been for someone thousands and thousands of years ago, back when saber-toothed tigers were alive.

Think of a man walking through a forest. Suddenly, he realizes he's being followed by a saber-toothed tiger (which is a lot bigger and fiercer than the tigers that exist now). He has a few choices to make, but he has to make them very quickly. He could **freeze** or play dead, but that might not work. He could **flee** (run away), but tigers are pretty fast runners. If he has something to use as a weapon, he could **fight** the tiger to protect himself. Also, if other people are close by, they might be able to help him. Whew! That's a lot of things he has to think about really quickly before the tiger makes a move!

Luckily, you and I don't come face to face with saber-toothed tigers like prehistoric people did!

Now, let's fast-forward to the present.

We don't have saber-toothed tigers walking down our streets, but we do face other situations that *feel* threatening. There could be bullies on the playground, hard tests and assignments, parents who get angry with us, and new people and places to figure out. Sometimes it can feel like we're in danger all the time, even when that's not really true.

Whether or not the danger is real, our **3F responses** (**fight**, **flight**, or **freeze**) can kick in because we really *feel* like we're in danger. This makes our inner caveperson come out!

When our worries get really big, our imagination might even come up with a really scary scene—like a movie in our mind—that makes the danger feel even more real.

Let's imagine what it might be like when our imagination makes a danger feel even bigger than it really is. Maybe there's a cute little dog, wagging her tail at you, but you *imagine* that she will bite you and that you'll end up hurt, bleeding, and in pain. Maybe you'll end up in the hospital, never able to come home. The whole scene you made up in your mind might feel like you're watching a scary movie. It can be pretty frightening, with lots of details that feel very real. But remember, all this is happening in your *imagination*. Really, that particular dog is very friendly and is still wagging her tail at you. Your body reacted to what was going on in your mind, not to what was actually happening.

That's how powerful your mind, and your imagination, can be!

Questions and Answers

When we worry, our mind and body don't just react to what's happening right now. They also react to things we remember from before. We can even imagine what might have happened, but didn't. We might even imagine things that could possibly happen, but are really, really unlikely.

When we remember, and imagine, all these scary things, we feel as if we're in danger. Then the **3F responses** kick in to protect us, just like they've been programmed to do.

There's something we can do when it feels like our imagination is helping our worries—really, there is! We can choose whether or not to imagine all these scary possibilities. After all, who is the boss of your mind? That's right…*you*! It's *your* mind and *your* imagination, and *you* can choose what direction you want them to go. It might take a little learning and practice, but this book is here to help you!

The Anxiety Workbook for Kids

Who Has Fears and Worries?

Everybody has some fears and worries. Parents, grandparents, teachers, brothers, sisters, and even other kids! They all have something that scares or worries them. Sometimes we get so stuck thinking about our own fears and worries that we don't even think about other people having them too.

You're not the only one who has fears and worries.

Pretend that you're a reporter. Interview someone in your family (or someone else you are comfortable with) about their fears and worries.

Interview Questions

Date:

Name:

Age:

Profession:

What makes you feel afraid or worried?

What have you told yourself about the worry and what could happen?

How did that make you feel?

What have you tried to help with that worry?

Was it helpful?

Other:

The Anxiety Workbook for Kids

Why Do Some People Worry More?

Sometimes people worry about real things. At those times, we can try to find the best solution. But lots of times, we end up worrying about things that are unlikely. Like monsters, our worries might not even be real or possible at all. Either way, since the mind is connected to the body, when we imagine something, our body has a response. This means that the stronger our **imagination** is, the more real these things can sometimes feel.

**Complete this quiz using yes or no answers
to see if you have a strong imagination.**

Imagination Quiz

1. Do you like to imagine the scenes from stories you read or hear?

2. Do you make up your own stories, even in your mind?

3. Do you like to draw or create other types of art?

4. Do you ever make up fun games or have creative ideas?

5. Do you ever have worries, even about things that aren't really happening or are unlikely to happen?

6. When you have worries, do you IMAGINE them in great detail? Kind of like a movie playing in your mind?

If you answered yes to any of these questions, then congratulations! You have a strong imagination. This is a great gift! Imagination is a powerful thing, and we can learn to be the boss of it, instead of feeling like it controls us. This book will help!

Put your name on the IMAGINATION badge. You've earned it by having a strong imagination! You can even use that imagination to help you deal with your worries.

What Is My Imagination Good For?

Sometimes our imagination can help our fears and worries, by getting us to imagine scary things to worry about. But it can also do a lot for us!

Is My Imagination Helping Me?

Take a look at some situations where your imagination might be involved.

Draw a star or put a sticker next to the situations where your imagination can be helpful.

Mark an X next to the situations where your imagination isn't so helpful.

Imagining things I like when I'm bored

Imagining the scene from a book I'm reading

Imagining my class laughing at me when I present my project

Imagining what I want to be when I grow up

Imagining how much fun I'll have at a party

Imagining getting a good grade if I work hard on a project

Imagining something bad happening to someone I care about

Imagining that a scene from a scary movie will happen in real life

Can I Become the Boss of My Imagination?

Learning to take charge of our imagination (especially when it seems to be helping our worries) may seem like a really big job. But, if we think about it, there are probably lots of things that we're good at now that used to seem nearly impossible.

Below are some things that other kids found hard but learned to do over time with practice, taking it one step at a time!

Circle any of the things below that you, or someone you know, can do now that took time and practice.

How do we learn new things? Let's look at the example of riding a bike.

To ride a bike, we need to learn how to balance and pedal at the same time. We also need to learn how to steer while moving forward so we don't fall over. Learning to train our imagination works in the same way. We need to learn to point our imagination in the direction we want it to go (steer), while giving it power to move forward (balance and pedal), just like a bike. Instead of letting our imagination go in a scary direction, we can use our imagination in safer, more relaxed, and even fun ways! Just like learning to ride a bike, we might have trouble and even crash a few times, but don't give up! These moments are part of the learning.

What Happens When We Hide Our Fears and Worries?

Lots of kids don't want other kids to know when they're afraid or worried. We can get pretty good at hiding our fears and worries when we want to. Here are some examples of how some other kids have hidden their fears and worries:

- **Not talking**

- **Distracting** themselves

- **Avoiding situations** where they might be noticed

- Putting a **blank look** on their face so their feelings don't show

- **Staying near people** they feel comfortable with

- **Letting other people speak** for them

Have you used any of these strategies?

Circle the strategies you have tried.

How did they work for you?

Can you think of any other ways people might hide their fears or worries from other people?

Write them here.

_____

_____

The Anxiety Workbook for Kids

Some of these strategies might seem to help in the moment because they make our worries seem smaller (at least until we face the same situation again). But sometimes there is a price to pay for using one of these strategies. For example, we might miss out on things that we would otherwise enjoy. By taking charge of our worries, we get to enjoy more things in life!

What Can We Do with Our Fears and Worries?

Often, because our fears and worries make us feel uncomfortable, we *imagine* that we would like to get rid of them. But these are normal feelings and can actually be quite healthy.

A small amount of fear and worry can actually help us. It helps us stay safe from things that could be real dangers to us, such as approaching a wild animal or touching a hot stove. A little bit of worry or anxiety about certain things, like homework or cleaning our room, can help us get things done. A little fear or worry can *motivate* or *push us to do something.* But, our fears and worries can cause problems for us if they get in the way of enjoying life.

Instead of getting rid of worries, we can find ways to **learn to manage our fears and worries**. We want them to work for us and not get in the way of enjoying life and having fun.

Chapter 2

Getting to Know More About Me

Getting to Know More About Me

Things I'm Already Good At

We all have things that we're good at. Sometimes these things come naturally, and sometimes they're things we practiced and became good at over time.

List or draw some of the things you are already good at on this page.

If you have trouble thinking of things, ask someone who knows you well what they appreciate about you.

A lot of these things probably took a lot of hard work and practice to learn. The ideas you'll learn about in this book will be fun, but will take some work and practice, too. Stick with it and this will get easier too!

I'm More than My Worries

Fears, worries, and anxiety are only a part of your life. You have so many other parts and experiences in your life. How much of your life is really filled with fear, worry, and anxiety?

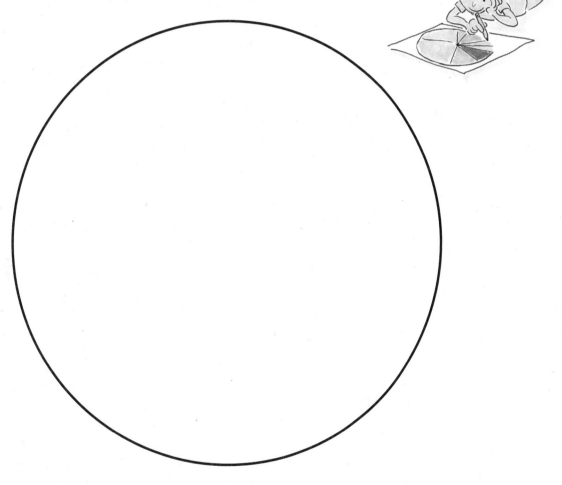

Pretend that everything in your life fits into this circle. Use colours, words, and/or pictures to show how much of your life is filled up with different things—family, friends, school, activities, and interests. Don't forget to show where fear, worry, and anxiety fit in, but also include your other feelings, like happiness, sadness, anger, excitement, or any others you've noticed.

Chapter 3

Getting To Know More About Fears and Worries

Common Fears and Worries

When we know what our fears and worries are, we can get ready to deal with them. Let's start by thinking about some common fears and worries.

Find the words from the list on the right in the word search below.

V	T	A	L	O	O	H	C	S	B	Y	B	I	C	N
Q	S	L	A	N	I	M	I	R	C	K	U	I	L	L
M	O	N	S	T	E	R	S	T	O	R	M	S	O	H
N	K	H	T	I	E	J	G	N	I	Y	L	F	W	E
O	G	E	R	M	S	L	O	H	T	A	E	D	N	I
I	N	D	V	I	N	S	E	C	T	S	F	T	S	G
T	E	T	E	S	T	S	C	V	A	S	R	H	I	H
A	C	C	I	D	E	N	T	S	A	I	K	W	C	T
R	I	E	D	V	Z	D	H	P	D	T	R	B	A	S
A	X	J	W	A	N	I	M	A	L	S	O	M	R	A
P	C	B	S	E	I	L	L	U	B	E	W	R	S	L
E	S	C	A	L	A	T	O	R	S	B	E	A	S	O
S	F	W	O	D	S	M	R	A	L	A	M	L	F	N
C	O	S	S	E	N	K	R	A	D	F	O	P	T	E
X	G	N	C	U	H	Z	F	V	O	C	H	P	W	L

ACCIDENTS
ALARMS
ALONE
ANIMALS
BULLIES
CARS
CLOWNS
CRIMINALS
DARKNESS
DEATH
DIRT
ELEVATORS
ESCALATORS
FLYING
GERMS
HEIGHTS
HOMEWORK
INSECTS
MONSTERS
SCHOOL
SEPARATION
STORMS
TESTS

Now, from the list, circle the fears and worries that trouble you the most.

Can you think of any common fears or worries that weren't in the word search?

Write them down or draw them here.

Learning About My Fears and Worries

It's important to get to know the things we worry about and how we react or respond to them. Once we realize that we're feeling afraid or worried, we can think about what to do to deal with those feelings. The activities in this book will help you do this.

In this book, you'll answer some questions that will help you get to know your fears and worries better. That way, you can learn to deal with them in a way that makes you feel safer and more confident! A lot of these questions can seem hard at first, but there are no right or wrong answers. No one knows *you* better than you—just do your best!

The Anxiety Workbook for Kids

My Fears and Worries

Draw or write about some of your worries here.

Getting to Know More About Fears & Worries

When Are My Worries Around?

There are some situations when our fears and worries are more likely to show up.

Draw or write about those situations here.

=

Worry Time

Sometimes, even when nothing is happening, we might feel anxious. It can seem like whenever our mind has some free space, we fill that space with worry.

What Are Body Clues?

When we start to feel worried or anxious, we might notice some changes, or reactions, in our body. Sometimes our body might tell us that we feel anxious before our mind does, which is why we call these reactions **body clues**.

Sometimes we might notice these body clues. When we do, we can use them as signals to think about ways to deal with whatever is making us feel worried or anxious.

Let's learn a little bit more about body clues—after you get to know them, you can begin to notice them more easily!

I KNOW ME BEST!

Getting to Know More
About Fears & Worries

Common Body Clues

These are some of the ways our body can react when we feel worried:

- crying

- wide eyes

- headache

- dizziness

- tight jaw

- tight muscles

- feeling shaky

- racing heartbeat

- faster or slower breathing

- feeling hot

- feeling cold

- numb or tingly fingers or toes

- sick stomach

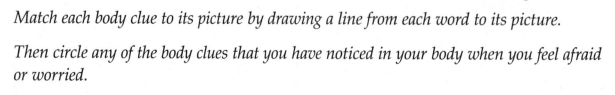

Match each body clue to its picture by drawing a line from each word to its picture.

Then circle any of the body clues that you have noticed in your body when you feel afraid or worried.

The Anxiety Workbook for Kids

What Is Happening in My Body?

Remember how our body adapted to danger by coming up with the **3F responses**, fight, flight, or freeze? Our body has some more reactions, or body clues, that help protect us and keep us safe. These reactions can even support the **3Fs**.

Let's look at some of the **things that happen in our body when we sense danger**. You may notice that we often experience these body clues at times when really big feelings, like worry, are around.

Let's use **Rico's story** as an example.

Rico walks onto the schoolyard and sees Lou heading his way. Rico knows that Lou can be a bully sometimes, so he expects Lou to pick on him. In other words, Rico immediately senses danger and begins to imagine the terrible things that might happen.

Let's think about the messages Rico's brain might send to the different parts of his body, and what he's feeling in his body right now.

Write down any ideas you have about what might be happening in Rico's mind or body.

Turn the page to see what can happen in our body when we feel anxiety.

Getting to Know More About Fears & Worries

The Brain and the Body

Let's look at some of the different messages our brain sends to our body and how our body reacts to those messages. When we worry, our body can feel like it's in danger. Our body has lots of ways it can get ready for action when we feel like we're in danger.

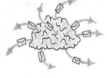

BRAIN

Message: "Get those messages out to the body! We have to protect ourselves!"

What Happens: Our brain sends out messages to the rest of our body to let it know what it needs to do. Because so much is going on in our mind and body while this is happening, we can sometimes get a headache.

EYES

Message: "Make sure you can see anything that might be dangerous."

What Happens: Our eyes widen, and our pupils (the black dot in the middle of our eyes that controls how much light gets in) sometimes get bigger or smaller. When our pupils get bigger, they let in the most amount of light so we can see everything. When they get smaller, they limit the amount of light to help us focus on one thing.

The Anxiety Workbook for Kids

MUSCLES

Message: "Get ready—we may have to move or defend ourselves."

What Happens: Our muscles often feel tense or tight as our body gets ready to defend itself or run. This can even happen to the muscles in our face or jaw, which causes us to clench our teeth.

LUNGS

Message: "Breathe! We need to be ready to send oxygen to our muscles."

What Happens: Our lungs often start to breathe faster and more deeply. This helps us get more oxygen to our muscles. Our muscles will need more oxygen to move more quickly if we need to defend ourselves or run. This is what sometimes makes us feel dizzy.

STOMACH

Message: "Stop digesting food. We have more important things to do right now!"

What Happens: Our brain knows that digesting food isn't as important as protecting ourselves when we feel like we're in danger, so it stops digesting food until we feel calm again. This can leave a lump of undigested food in our stomach, which can give us a stomachache or make us feel sick.

HEART

Message: "Hurry up, heart! Our muscles might need more blood quickly!"

What Happens: Our heart starts to pump faster, sending oxygen in our blood to our bigger muscles. Our muscles need oxygen to give them energy to defend ourselves or run. We might feel like our heart is racing, and sometimes we can even hear our heartbeat thumping in our ears!

BLOOD

Message: "Move to any big muscles that might need you! They need you more than those little areas."

What Happens: Because our blood is moving to our big muscles, the smaller areas of our body, like our hands and feet, get less blood. Our hands and feet might feel cold, numb, or tingly, while other areas, like our face and chest, might feel hot and get red. Sometimes this even makes us feel shaky all over.

SKIN

Message: "Cool down!"

What Happens: Our body starts to sweat to cool itself down in case we need to start running or use a lot of energy.

The picture on the next page shows what these body clues can look like.

People often notice some of these **body clues** when they feel worried, but it can feel different for everyone.

When we notice what happens in our body when we're anxious or worried, we can find a way to deal with our worries more quickly! Keep reading to learn ways to help relax your mind and body when anxiety is around.

Getting to Know More About Fears & Worries

My Body Clues

Before we learn even more about body clues, think about some of your body clues that you might have noticed before.

Draw Your Body Clues

Draw what happens in your body when you feel afraid or worried.

Don't worry about getting the "right" answers. What feels right for you is all that matters. You are the expert on you!

Chapter 4

Taking Charge of
My Mind and Body

My Skills and Strategies

List or draw any strategies you've tried to help you deal with your fears or worries.

Circle those that have been helpful.

Then rate each strategy on a scale of 0 to 5, with 0 being "not helpful at all" and 5 being "the most helpful." Write your rating next to each strategy.

The Anxiety Workbook for Kids

My Very Own Worry Box

Sometimes it can feel as though worry wants to be around ALL THE TIME. It's not a good idea to let worry completely take over, because it can get in the way of other important things we need to do, like eating, sleeping, doing homework, and even playing and having fun!

We need to be able to take a break from worry. To do that, we need a place to put it. As we get older, we learn to put things away in imaginary sections in our mind to come back to later. Sometimes it even helps to imagine these different sections as actual places, like drawers or files, where we keep different things to think about later. While we learn to do this, it can help to make a *real* place to keep our worry, where we know we can come back and deal with it later. To do this, lots of kids make a **worry box**.

Turn the page to learn how to make your very own worry box!

Taking Charge of My Mind and Body

To make your very own worry box, first get any box that's small enough to easily keep around, but big enough to put pieces of paper inside. An old shoebox or tissue box works great. Since you want to be able to put the worries in and take them out, the box should have a way to open and close, like a cover or flap. You can decorate this box however you want—try using construction paper, markers, crayons, or stickers! Some kids even like to imagine that the box has special materials, powers, or protections that keep the worries in.

To use the worry box, draw or write down a worry on a piece of paper and put it inside the worry box any time you have a worry that you're not ready to deal with yet. This could be when you're trying to sleep or to focus on schoolwork. When you're ready, you can take the worry out of the box and think of the skills and strategies you have to help you deal with that worry. This book will help you come up with lots of ways you can deal with your worries. You can even get someone close to you to help if you want!

Some Things Other Kids Found Helpful

You probably already have a lot of strategies you're really good at, and you might have some pretty good ideas for dealing with fears and worries.

Keep doing all the things you already find helpful!

You might also want to try some **strategies that other kids have found helpful.**

Doing activities that help you relax

Thinking positive thoughts

Talking about your thoughts and feelings

Standing up for yourself

Problem solving

Facing fears one step at a time

Being the boss of your own imagination!

You might have already tried some similar ideas, and some of them might be new to you. You can decide which ideas work best for you—you might even want to use different strategies for different situations.

Before deciding just how helpful these ideas are, be sure to **practice** them! Just like we can't jump on a bike and ride it right away without practicing, a lot of kids find that they need to practice before these ideas start to be really helpful.

Check off any ideas in the list that you tried and found helpful.

Chapter 4

Taking Charge of My Mind and Body

Mind and Body Training: Relaxation and Mindfulness

There are things we can do to help us relax. Sometimes, we do them without even thinking, like taking a deep breath when we feel stressed. Other times, we might plan to do things that we find relaxing.

People have different ideas about what is or isn't relaxing, and that's okay!

Some ways of relaxing might help relax the **mind,** while others focus more on the **body**. Because our mind and body are connected, relaxing one can help relax the other too!

My Relaxation Ideas

Draw or list some things you already do that help you relax.

Then rate each strategy on a scale of 0 to 5, with 0 being "not helpful at all" and 5 being "the most helpful." Write your rating next to each strategy.

Taking Charge of My Mind and Body

The Body Stress Test

1.   Lie on your bed.

2.   Lift one arm up in front of you.

3.   Let it drop.

4.   See if your muscles tighten to catch your arm.

5.   If your muscles tightened, completely relax your arm and try it again.

6.   Repeat this with your other arm.

7.   Now, do this with each of your legs.

As you do the **Body Stress Test**, you might notice that it's easier to let your muscles go when you feel relaxed. Try doing this test when you want to know if your body needs to relax!

The Anxiety Workbook for Kids

The Body Scan

Let's see if there are any tight spots in your body. You can imagine scanning your body from head to toe while you sit comfortably in a chair. Imagine that you are using a special muscle ray scanner...*bzzzzzzzzzz*. Starting at your head, check every muscle in your body, all the way down to your toes. Completely relax every muscle as the scanner passes it, and notice how different it feels when your muscles are loose. You might not have even realized that some of your muscles were tight to begin with!

1. Scan your **forehead**, then your **cheeks**.

2. Move down to your **neck**.

3. Let your **head** drop forward softly.

4. Feel your **shoulders** droop when the scanner passes over them.

5. Allow your **arms** and **hands** to drop gently to your sides.

6. Let your **belly** relax when the scanner passes.

7. Breathe all the air out of your **lungs** before taking another breath.

8. As you move your attention down your body, notice your **hips** and **legs** relax.

9. Now, your **feet**. You can even wiggle your **toes** a little and feel how the muscles loosen up.

Any time you think your body might be tight, you can do a body scan. Not only will it help you see if you're tight or loose, but it can help you relax, too!

Taking Charge of My Mind and Body

My Relaxation List

Now, try some of the relaxation activities on the following pages. It's a good idea to practice these regularly so you'll feel comfortable using them when you need them most.

Circle the ones you find most helpful as you try them!

As you find other strategies that help you relax, write them down in your own **relaxation list:**

The Anxiety Workbook for Kids

Deep Belly Breathing

You can use **deep belly breathing** to signal to your body that it's time to relax.

First, get into a comfortable position—you can sit or lie down, as long as all your muscles can relax. Close your eyes if you want to. Pay attention to your breathing for a few minutes. In, out, in, out…

Now, slow down and relax your breathing. Take long, slow breaths. In, out, in, out…

Next, to make sure you're taking full **belly breaths**, place one hand on your belly. Feel your belly filling up round like a balloon as you breathe in. Your belly should raise up higher than your chest. This kind of breathing helps you take deeper breaths.

Breathe in through your nose as you fill up your belly, and out through your lips as you breathe out. Notice the cool air going in through your nose and the warm air going out through your mouth. Let your muscles relax as your breath leaves through your lips.

Continue to slow down your breathing. Count slowly while you take slow, deep breaths in. Hold your breath, then count slowly while you breathe out in a relaxed way. Don't worry about how high you can count. Slow and steady is best. Do this for a few minutes until you feel calm and relaxed.

Taking Charge of My Mind and Body

Muscle Relaxation: A Trip to the Circus

Relaxing our muscles can help us relax our mind and our body.

To relax our **body**, we practice tightening and relaxing our muscles. This can help us notice how our body feels different when our muscles are tight or relaxed. And that can help us learn how to loosen up those tight muscles!

To relax our **mind**, we focus our mind, especially our **imagination**, on things that are calming, or even fun!

The first few times you try this exercise, it might help to have someone read it aloud for you so you can be free to just imagine. The person reading to you can also act it out with you.

First, choose a color that you think matches the feeling of worry.

Worry color: _____

Now, choose a color that helps you feel calm and relaxed.

Calm, relaxed color: _____

In the next exercise, you're going to **imagine** the feelings in your body as these different colors. Using your **imagination**, you're going to try to change your whole body from the worry color to your calm, relaxed color.

The Anxiety Workbook for Kids

Start by imagining that your body is completely filled up with the **worry color**. In a few moments, you will start to tighten and relax every group of muscles one by one, starting at your feet and moving up your body. You can imagine the color of those muscles changing to the **calm, relaxed color** as they loosen up. When you get to the top of your head, you'll push that worried color right up and out of your body, leaving you with only the calm, relaxed color—from head to toe!

You can even imagine that the calm, relaxed color brings a **comfortable, relaxing temperature** with it. Do you prefer to be warm or cool? You get to choose!

To help you practice in a fun way, we're going to imagine that we're at the circus. Sit in a chair with your feet on the floor. Make sure you feel comfortable. Take relaxed belly breaths, closing your eyes if you want to.

As you do the different activities, feel free to open your eyes and get up and act them out! Remember, this circus only exists in your imagination, so it's a totally safe place. You control what happens there. You even get to decide if you want to bring anyone with you!

Taking Charge of My Mind and Body

Now, imagine that you just arrived early to the circus, so you sit on a bench to wait. It was raining earlier and the ground is a little wet and muddy. You're wearing old rain boots, so you decide to **smoosh your feet** into the mud.

You smoosh your feet around for a while and notice that when you try to pull your feet out of the mud, they're a little stuck. When you smoosh your feet deep into the mud, you can push them hard against the solid ground underneath the mud. **Spread your toes** out as wide as you can. Then, curl your toes up tight into a ball. Notice how tight your feet feel with your toes curled up. Now, wiggle your feet around and shake them to loosen them up. Tighten and relax your toes a few times. When the muscles in your feet feel loose, imagine that they have filled up with your calm, relaxing color. Just as you finish squishing your feet around in the mud, the circus gates open and you go in.

After you go inside, you notice a goalie game that looks fun. You think you might be pretty good at it, so you give it a try. You stand in front of the net and get ready to block the soccer balls. You notice that the game first aims the ball at the right side of the net, and on the next turn, it aims at the left side of the net. This means you can get ready by lifting your **right leg** out to the side when you know the ball is coming to the right side of the net. Hold your right leg out for a few seconds, keeping the muscles tight, so you can block the ball. Keep your toes up, too—that way, you can block the most space. Feel those muscles getting tight. It worked! You blocked the ball. Now, try it again with the left leg. Notice how tight this leg is compared to the one that you just relaxed.

You still have four more balls coming! Repeat this exercise twice for the right leg and twice for the left leg. Pay attention to how tight your leg muscles are when you're getting ready to block the ball compared to how relaxed they are when you let the muscles relax. Then, shake your leg muscles loose and imagine that calm, relaxing color rising from your feet to fill your leg muscles. Now your calm, relaxed color goes all the way up to your knees.

Next, you decide to go into the big tent to look around. The circus performers are practicing, and one performer is talking to a crowd of kids sitting around him on chairs. There's space for you to join them. The performer is describing what it's like to be shot out of a cannon. He explains that he has to curl up tight and small into a ball to get into the right position.

He invites you to see how small you can curl up in your chair. Pull your **legs** right up to your **chest,** wrapping your **arms** around them. Squeeze your **thighs** in to help you get even smaller. Now, you're in a tight ball. Notice how it feels to be so tight. The performer tells you to imagine shooting out of the cannon. Release your legs and hop out of the chair, stretching your arms out as you imagine shooting out of the cannon. Feel all those muscles relax as you imagine flying through the air. Try it again one more time.

All the muscles you used to curl into a tight ball are feeling a little looser now. Imagine your calm, relaxed color filling up those muscles, through your thighs and hips, and beginning to trickle up your body to your shoulders. The performers need to practice some more, so everyone starts to leave the tent to see the other attractions.

Taking Charge of My Mind and Body

As you leave the tent, you realize some of the gates out of the tent are already closed. You decide to squeeze through one gate that has been left open a little. Suck in your **belly** as tight as you can to squeeze through the gate sideways. As you inch all the way through while keeping your belly sucked in, you notice how your belly feels when it's all tightened up. Once you're through, let your belly go loose. Then, take a deep breath and hold it for a second before letting it out—it feels so good to take a full breath! Just then, a breeze snatches your ticket out of your hand and blows it to the ground just inside the gate. Now you have to squeeze back through. Again, feel how tight your belly becomes when you suck it in, and how relaxed it feels when you make it through the gate and let your muscles go. Now, go back through the gate one more time. By now, your belly feels super relaxed. Imagine your belly filling up with your calm, relaxing color.

Now that you're back outside the tent, you see a lemon-squeezing contest. You decide to challenge yourself to see how quickly you can squeeze the juice out of the lemons. Before you start, stretch to get ready. Join your hands together in front of you and push forward. Now, move your hands up over your head and back as far as you can, still holding your hands together. Next, hold your hands together behind your back and push them out. Notice how tight your **arms**, **shoulders**, and **back** feel. Let go and shake all those muscles loose. Feel your calm, relaxing color trickling up your body, filling your back and shoulders.

Now, time for the lemons! You get two lemons, one for each of your **hands**. Pick up those lemons and squeeze them as hard as you can! Squeeze tight! Your hands might even change color, looking white in some places and red in others. Now, stop squeezing. Drop those lemons and shake out your hands. Notice how different your hands feel when they're relaxed and loose compared to how tight they were when you were squeezing. Now that your hands have had a break, let's get back to squeezing. There is still some juice left in those lemons. Squeeze! Squeeze! Squeeze! Feel how tight you're squeezing. Now relax. You've squeezed out enough juice to win a prize! You notice that your calm, relaxed color has spread to your hands and lower arms.

Next, you see two bodybuilders in the crowd, taking pictures with people. You want to get a picture with them, too! They invite you to flex your **upper arms** for the picture. Flex your right arm as hard as you can. Reach over with your left hand and feel your muscle all tensed up. Now, relax your right arm and flex your left upper arm. Touch it with your right hand. For the final picture, you decide to flex both arms at once, before relaxing them and shaking them out. How much of your body is filled with your calm, relaxed color now?

Then, you notice a reptile tent and decide to stop and take a look. You see a turtle slowly duck its head inside its shell, and you start to imagine what it would be like to be a turtle. Pull your **shoulders** up slowly, while pulling your **head** into your shell at the same time. Imagine hiding in there where it's nice and protected. Now, poke your head out slowly to see if it's safe out there. Lift your head straight up as far as you can while you let your shoulders back down. Now, slowly like a turtle, look to the right, then to the left, then straight ahead. What would you do if you saw a large bird? Hide inside your shell again, pulling your shoulders up and your head straight down. Now, peek out again—bring your head back up, looking to the right, then the left, then center. Lift your face up to the sky to make sure the bird is gone. You're safe! Now, your calm, relaxed color fills you all the way up to the top of your neck.

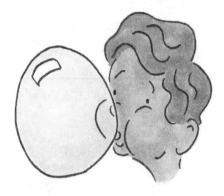

Next, you decide to join a bubble-blowing competition. Imagine that you have a piece of gum that's bigger than any piece of gum you have ever chewed. Chew as hard as you can to get the gum ready to blow bubbles. Move the gum around. Feel it stretch your **cheeks**. Now, spit it out and take a break. Relax your cheeks. Push on them with your hands to feel how loose they are. Now, chew your gum again. It's time to blow your big bubble! BLOW! Watch the bubble grow bigger and bigger, until... POP! The bubble pops, right on top of your nose. Pull it off and throw it away. You blew a really big bubble and won a ribbon! You also notice that your **jaw** and cheeks are filled with your calm, relaxed color now.

A small fly lands on your nose—it likes the sugar left on your face from the bubble gum! You don't want to use your hands to get the fly off because they are still sticky from the gum. You decide to wiggle your **nose** to get it off! Wiggle, wiggle...the fly is gone! You can relax now. But wait...here comes the fly again. Wiggle hard! Okay, it's gone. You can relax. But...oh no! Here comes another one! One more time...wiggle that nose! The fly flies over to the cotton candy stand and leaves you alone, and you can relax your **face**. Imagine that someone gives you a facecloth to wash your face. Scrunch up your face as you wash it. Imagine taking the time to enjoy smooshing your face muscles around with your hands. Imagine that the last little bit of the worried color is leaving your face. That color has now been pushed all the way up and out of your body—from your toes all the way up through the top of your head!

The Anxiety Workbook for Kids

How do you feel after tightening and relaxing all of your muscles?

Even though you learned to tighten and relax your muscles by imagining a fun trip to the circus, you can tense and relax your muscles at any time, no matter where you are.

Use this checklist to help you remember each body part:

☐ **toes and feet** (mud)

☐ **lower legs** (goalie game)

☐ **thighs and hips** (cannon)

☐ **belly** (gate)

☐ **back and shoulders** (stretch)

☐ **lower arms and hands** (lemon-squeezing competition)

☐ **upper arms** (bodybuilders)

☐ **neck and shoulders** (turtle)

☐ **jaw and cheeks** (bubble-blowing competition)

☐ **nose** (fly)

☐ **face** (washing your face)

Making a Stress Ball

Have you ever squeezed a **stress ball**? A stress ball can be any small, squishy ball that you can squeeze in your hand. You can buy stress balls at any dollar store, but it's also really easy to make your own.

What You Need:

- **Two balloons**: Make sure one of the balloons is a favorite color or has a fun picture (such as a happy face) on it. You'll be able to see this balloon when your stress ball is finished.

- **Filling for the balloons**: Flour or cornstarch works well, but you can also use rice, beads, or dried beans.

- **Funnel**: This needs to fit inside the neck of the balloon.

Steps:

1. Place the funnel in the neck of one balloon (not the balloon you want on the outside).

2. Slowly pour small amounts of the filling into the funnel. Give the funnel a little shake to help the filling flow through the funnel's hole into the balloon. If the filling gets stuck, use a pencil to push it through.

3. After filling the balloon, remove the funnel and tie the balloon.

4. Ask someone to hold the opening of your second balloon open. It helps if they put two fingers of each hand into the neck of the balloon and pull. Place the filled balloon inside, and then tie off the second balloon.

Now, you have your very own stress ball. Give it a squeeze and try it out!

You can carry your stress ball with you and squeeze it any time you need to relax.

Taking Charge of My Mind and Body

Creating My Own Peaceful Place

You're going to imagine your own **peaceful, safe place** that you can visit in your mind any time you want to relax. You get to decide everything about this place: where it is, what it's like, whether anyone is with you, and what you **see, smell, hear, taste,** and **feel**.

First, relax your body and get in a comfortable position. Try to calm your mind and body by focusing on your breathing. Breathe in and out slowly, letting your breathing relax you. Breathe in…hold…and let it out slowly. Pay attention to your breathing… slow, calm, and gentle. As your heartbeat slows down, your body gets more and more relaxed.

Next, start to imagine a place where you would feel completely relaxed and peaceful!

Let's start with where this place is. Is it a place in nature or indoors? A big, open place or a small, cozy one? Does your place look like somewhere in this world, or is it in a made-up world? Keep imagining what this place looks like. What do you **see** around you? What are the colors? Are there any plants, animals, or other living things?

Are you **alone** in this peaceful place, or would you like to have some company with you? Since this is *your* place in *your* mind, you get to choose everything. This place is completely safe!

Now, notice what **time** of day it is. What is the light like? Is it bright or dark? What's the temperature? Is it cool? Comfortable? Warm? Is there a breeze, or is the air still and calm?

Taking Charge of My Mind and Body

Can you **hear** anything? If you're outside, do you hear waves crashing, or birds chirping? Are you indoors listening to your favorite band? Or is it calm and silent?

Take a deep breath in through your nose. What do you **smell**? Are there nature smells? Food smells? Maybe you can smell some of your favorite things, like flowers or fresh, clean laundry.

Now imagine whether you **taste** anything in your peaceful place. Is there anything you would like to be eating or drinking?

What are you doing in your peaceful place? Are you sitting or lying down, relaxing somewhere comfortable? Or, are you doing any **activities**? Walking around? Floating? Flying? Is there anything else you might enjoy doing there?

Imagine what you **feel** with your body. What is your skin touching? Are you holding anything? If so, what does it feel like?

Keep enjoying your peaceful place. Notice all the different things you can **see, smell, hear, taste,** and **feel**.

Know that this place will stay safe inside your imagination and you can visit it any time you need to relax. It's like a free vacation, and you don't even need to pack a suitcase! Even as you return to your day, know that you can take that calm, peaceful feeling with you.

Notes on My Peaceful Place:

Where am I? What is this place like?

What do I see?

Is anyone with me? If so, who?

What time of day is it?

What's the temperature?

What do I hear?

What do I smell?

What do I taste?

What am I doing?

What do I feel against my body?

Any other important details?

Taking Charge of My Mind and Body

Draw a picture of your peaceful place.

Mindfulness Meditation

Being **mindful** is being aware of the moment you're in—at that moment.

We can get distracted by a lot of things. Sometimes we think about things that have already happened. Or, we might be busy looking ahead to the future, and maybe even worrying about it. We can spend a lot of our time worrying about things that haven't even happened yet (and may never happen) rather than being aware of the moment we're in. When we are mindful, we notice what's happening right now! We can really appreciate things that we sometimes miss out on.

But, being mindful might also mean letting ourselves notice what we're feeling, even when our feelings are unpleasant. Lots of times, people try to push tough feelings away. It makes sense—tough feelings are hard to have around. And let's face it, we even worry about having worries! But when we try to push our feelings away without facing them, they often end up sticking around or popping back up when we don't expect it. Sometimes they're even stronger than before! It can actually be more helpful to just notice (and accept) our tough feelings as we feel them. Even though it can be hard work, it can help us be more relaxed and not be scared of our feelings, instead of worrying about how to get rid of them.

To be more mindful, take some time each day to sit with your eyes closed and just notice your thoughts, your feelings, your body (including all of your senses— sight, touch, hearing, smell, and taste), and your environment (everything around you).

Taking Charge of My Mind and Body

Take a moment and try to meditate…

First, find a comfortable place to sit. Lots of people choose to sit cross-legged on the floor with their back straight up. You can use a cushion if you want to.

Then, close your eyes and just focus on your breathing for a little while. Feel free to take your time. You can stop at each step as long as you want.

Take a few moments to notice how fast or slow your breath is.

Next, without opening your eyes, bring your attention to the room around you. Do you hear any sounds? Does the room smell like anything? From behind your eyelids, does the room seem light or dark? Do you feel anything against your body? How does the floor (or the surface you're on) feel?

Next, notice your body all over. Notice if your muscles are tight or loose. Feel free to let any tight muscles relax. Every now and then, go back to noticing your breathing.

You'll probably notice some thoughts will come into your mind. Don't worry about making your mind blank. You can notice your thoughts, and your feelings too. Try your best not to decide whether they are good thoughts or bad thoughts—just notice that they're there. No thought or feeling will last forever. They will all come and go, even if some might come back.

If you notice a feeling that is really difficult, like a worry, try not to push it away. All of your feelings are a part of you. Remember that you're safe where you are sitting meditating. Try to sit with that worry and focus on your breathing again. You've probably noticed that when you try to push a worry away it often comes back, but when you can learn to sit with a worry you can start to feel more calm and confident when it's around.

Keep noticing your breathing, taking a full, deep breath when it feels good. Keep noticing your body in general, your thoughts, your feelings and your mood, and the world around you.

Take a few moments, and when you're ready, open your eyes and return to your day.

If you do this regularly, it can help you notice more about yourself and the world around you, and you might find that difficult thoughts and feelings don't seem as strange and scary as they once did.

The Anxiety Workbook for Kids

Taking Charge of My Mind and Body

Bubble Meditation

This **bubble meditation** can help you slow down and notice your thoughts, your feelings, and even what's going on in your body, without getting stuck on any one thing. When we don't spend a lot of time holding on to these things, we have more time for noticing other things, too!

First, get comfortable. Sit up with your back straight but relaxed. Try to let go of any tightness in your muscles (give them a little wiggle to loosen them up if you have to), and start with some deep belly breathing.

Now, imagine that bubbles slowly start to float up in front of you, one at a time. They start from the floor and float up through the ceiling (or into the sky if you're outside) until you can't see them anymore. Inside each bubble, picture one of your thoughts, or feelings, or even something you're noticing. You can picture something that's on your mind, such as the fight you had with your best friend, or how you're feeling right now. You can even picture something you're feeling in your body, such as having an itchy nose. Some bubbles might be empty, or some might have the same thought or feeling over and over again. That's okay—let your bubbles fill up with whatever comes to mind, and then watch them float away.

Now, notice a new bubble right in front of you. Look at what's inside and then watch it slowly float up and away like the others. Try not to think of what's inside the bubble as being "good" or "bad." Just look at what's inside the bubble, without thinking more about it. Watch it as it floats away. Keep watching your bubbles float away for a few more minutes while using your deep belly breathing, until they're all gone. Keep breathing comfortably, and when you're ready, open your eyes again. How was that?

If you practice just noticing thoughts and feelings like this, it might not feel so scary when they're around. It can also help to realize that lots of different thoughts and feelings come and go, and even if some do come back for a bit, there are other moments, thoughts, and feelings to notice too.

Brain Breathing

Even though our brain doesn't really "breathe," we're going to learn a way to imagine our brain breathing in fresh, clean air and breathing out dark, heavy air. Let's start with regular deep belly breathing. First, just breathe regularly, then slow down and concentrate on bringing deep, full breaths into your belly and letting the breaths out through your mouth.

Now, as you breathe in, imagine fresh, cool air flowing up into your head and swirling around your brain. This time, instead of breathing out through your mouth, let the air flow back out through your nose. With your next breath in, imagine the air collecting any worries with it and pulling them back out through your nose as it exits. Fresh, cool air in. Worry-filled air out.

With the next breath in, imagine the air getting a little stronger, but still gentle, like a swirling wind. Imagine the air coming in, gathering up anything heavy or dark in your brain. Now, imagine the heavy, dark air escaping through your nose and your ears this time. It can't get back in, and the only thing left behind is clean, light air. If you have a headache, imagine that being pulled out, too.

Continue to breathe this way until you imagine that all your worries, darkness, or pain have been pulled away, leaving only a light, clear mind.

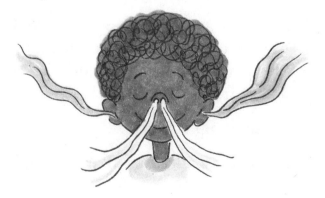

Making a Feeling Jar

When we have a lot of worries racing and buzzing around in our mind, it can be really hard to calm them down. To help us settle them down, we can make a **feeling jar**!

What You Need:

- **A plastic, see-through jar:** A small, travel-sized shampoo bottle works well, especially if you want to carry your feeling jar with you!

- **Sparkles and small beads or objects:** Try to gather lots of different colors for variety.

- **Water**

- **Glycerin or gel medium, or even glitter glue**

Steps:

1. Fill your jar most of the way with water, leaving a little space for sparkles. You can always add more water later if you need to.

2. Add a drop of glycerin, gel, or glitter glue. You can add more if you want the sparkles to move more slowly. Stir or shake the jar with the cover on.

3. Choose a different color for every worry swirling around in your mind. For worries that seem to come and go, choose heavier beads or objects in that color. For worries that really swirl around for a while, choose some sparkles. Put these in your jar.

4. Put on the cover and shake up your jar.

5. Imagine that the beads and sparkles are all the worries swirling around in your mind.

6. Watch the beads and sparkles while they settle down. You'll notice that some settle quickly, while others float around for a while.

7. Take deep belly breaths while you watch, until the last of the sparkles settles down.

8. Notice how much calmer you feel. Some worries will come back again in the future—that's part of life—but now you know how to help them settle down. For now, you can leave your worries settled in the jar and keep that calm feeling with you!

Taking Charge of My Thoughts

It's important to take time to notice all of our thoughts and feelings (including the tough ones), but it's also important to take time to notice the positive (good) things around us.

Sometimes it seems like our mind is really good at paying attention to all of the negative, scary things that happen (or could happen) around us. For example, if you have a test coming up, you might think **scary thoughts**, like "I'm never going to pass" or "I never get anything right."

But are those scary thoughts really true? Most likely, there are lots of things that you can do that you once worried were impossible. Just think about all those things you listed or drew in the *Things I'm Already Good At* section.

Some **positive thoughts** that kids have found helpful include:

- "If I could learn that, then I can learn this."

- "I'll do better with practice."

- "I can do this."

- "Just breathe and do your best."

If you realize you're thinking scary or negative thoughts, you can stand up to those thoughts with these **questions**:

- Is that really true?

- Does that always happen?

- Is it possible that this could turn out differently?

- What else might happen?

- What would I tell one of my friends if they were worried about this?

The Anxiety Workbook for Kids

Let's try this exercise. Below, put a ☑️ by the **positive thoughts**, put an X by the scary, **negative thoughts**, and <u>underline</u> the **questions** you could use to challenge yourself.

_____ I can only do my best.

_____ I'm not good at anything.

_____ I'll never get it.

_____ Is that really true?

_____ I'm good at lots of things.

_____ What advice would I give a friend?

The Worry Leap Frog Game

There are lots of things that happen that we can't control. There are things we have to do that we have no control over, like having to go to school or going with our family on vacation. We also can't control the words or actions of other people. But we *can* control what we think about things that are out of our control and how we react to them. When we change the way we think, it can change the way we feel about something, our choices, and what happens in the end!

The Worry Leap Frog Game will help you think about, and maybe change, the way you think so that you can enjoy more things in life.

Read the rules below. The example after that will help you to understand better before you try the game on your own.

Worry Leap Frog Game Rules:
1. Write down the **situation** that you're worried about.
2. Write down the **negative** or scary **thoughts** you have about the situation in the **thoughts** lily pad on the Worried Path.
3. Write down the **feeling** that goes with those thoughts in the **feelings** lily pad.
4. In the **actions** lily pad, write what you think you would do if you listened to the scary thoughts.
5. In the **outcomes** lily pad, write down the end result of your actions if you followed the Worried Path.
6. Repeat these steps for the Brighter Path. Remember, you can't change the situation, but you can change the thoughts you tell yourself about the situation. Notice how your feelings, your actions, and the outcome change when you notice some of the more positive things that you may have been missing before.

Look at the example, and then play the Worry Leap Frog Game on your own.

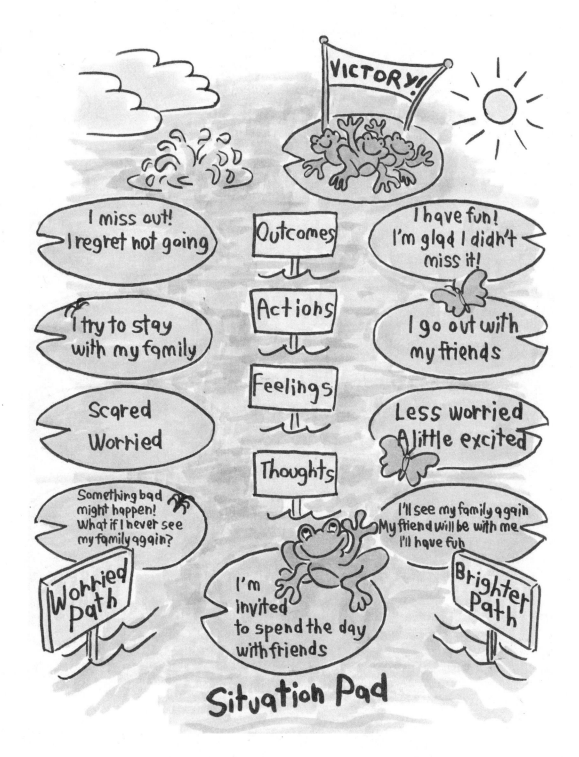

Taking Charge of My Mind and Body

The Anxiety Workbook for Kids

Act Positive to Feel Positive

We've learned about noticing and changing our thoughts to help us have more positive **emotions** (how we feel), **actions** (what we do), and **outcomes** (what happens in the end).

Now, let's think about how changing our **behavior** (actions) can also change the way we feel. For example, even if we're feeling worried about something, we can do something that we enjoy to lift our mood. It can even feel good just to be silly sometimes!

One way to be silly and lift our mood is to sing or whistle a happy tune. If you feel like you could use a pick-me-up, sing or whistle the happiest or silliest song you know. This helps your brain get into the mood you're usually in when you sing that song. If you can't think of a silly song, you can even try to make one up. We all need to take a break from our worries, and take the time to be silly sometimes!

Taking Charge of My Mind and Body

Talking to Others

We've learned that we can't always control situations or what other people do, but it's still important to let others know our **thoughts, feelings,** and **needs**. We might even need other people's help sometimes. If we don't tell people what we're thinking and feeling, it can be hard for them to understand what we need.

One way to express your thoughts and feelings is to use an "**I feel…when…**" sentence:

I feel _____ **when** _____ .
　　　　　　　(feeling) 　　　　　　　　　　　　　　　　　(situation)

Here's an example:

I feel worried **when** we go to a new place and I don't know what's going to happen.

If you already have an idea of what someone can do to help, you can add that information, too.

I feel worried **when** we go to a new place and I don't know what's going to happen. **It would help if** you could tell me what to expect.

Now you try it!

I feel _____ **when** _____ .

It would help if _____ .

Being Assertive (Standing Up for Myself)

The story below will help you understand three big words: **passive, aggressive,** and **assertive**.

When someone is being **passive**, it means that they might accept whatever happens without standing up for themselves, even when there's something that they still want or need.

When someone is being **aggressive**, they can seem pushy. It might look to others like they think what they want is more important than what other people want.

If someone is being **assertive**, they stand up for themselves and express their thoughts and feelings, but they're still considerate of other people's feelings. When people are assertive, they are often more confident and fair.

You'll read about three people in this story. Can you figure out who is being **passive**, who is acting **aggressively**, and who is being **assertive**?

It's lunchtime at school and Johnny is excited because it's Pizza Day. Hawaiian-style pizza is his favorite, and he's worried that it will be gone before he can get a slice. All of a sudden, Patrick cuts in front of him in the line.

Ugh…Patrick is always trying to get to the Hawaiian pizza first, Johnny thinks as he puts his hands in his pockets and looks at his feet. He wishes a teacher had seen Patrick cut in line and done something.

Just then, Johnny notices his older brother's friend, Jamal, rushing over. Jamal pushes Patrick out of the line and yells at him for cutting in front of Johnny.

Taking Charge of My Mind and Body

Johnny is relieved that Jamal stood up for him, but then he realizes that Mr. Williams saw Jamal push Patrick, and he's headed this way.

Jamal is sent to the office, even though he was standing up for his friend. Mr. Williams says that everyone is responsible for their own behavior no matter what the other person did first, and that Jamal could've helped in another way.

Mr. Williams talks to Johnny and Patrick and figures out why Jamal pushed Patrick. Mr. Williams reminds Patrick of the school rules on not cutting in line, and why it's important for everyone to follow the rules and be fair.

Even though Johnny feels nervous, Mr. Williams helps him tell Patrick how he felt when Patrick cut in front of him. Mr. Williams encourages Johnny to use an "I feel…when…" sentence. Johnny takes a deep belly breath and says, "Patrick, I feel sad and angry when you cut in front of me. It's not fair, and I like Hawaiian pizza just as much as you. You need to wait in line, too."

Johnny feels better because he said what was on his mind. Patrick goes to the back of the line and gets a warning that if he tries to cut in line again, he will have to stay for detention. Even with all the commotion, Johnny gets a slice of Hawaiian pizza! He feels pretty proud because he stood up for himself!

Who was being **passive** in this story? _____

Two people were acting **aggressively** in this story. Who were they? _____

_____

What happened to the people who were acting **aggressively**? _____

_____

Who was a support person (someone who helped)? _____

Who changed from acting in a **passive way** to being more **assertive** by the end of the story?

_____

What did that person do to be more **assertive**? _____

How did it help the situation? _____

Chapter 5

Taking Charge of Worries About Real Things

Taking Charge of Worries About Real Things

We've already learned that some of the things we worry about are more likely to happen than others. For example, we can't avoid taking tests at school, going to new places, and trying new things, even though we worry about them. There are also certain fears we have that we may want to get over, such as being around certain animals or ordering food at a restaurant.

We're going to focus on some strategies we can learn that will help us deal with real-life worries and fears.

One way to deal with real-life worries is to practice ways to **keep ourselves safe**, such as wearing a seatbelt, keeping doors locked, and being cautious around strange animals you don't know. The adults in your life might even remind you to do these things.

Also, when we find ourselves in hard situations that we aren't sure how to handle, such as dealing with a bully, we can use **problem-solving steps** to help us find the best solution.

Finally, when we're worried about trying new things or we have a fear that we want to overcome, we can make a **step-by-step plan** and practice one step at a time. Let's learn how!

Problem Solving

We all face tough problems sometimes. We solve problems every day. Some are smaller, like deciding which topic to pick for an assignment, and some are bigger. You probably have more experience with solving problems than you even realize.

When problems happen, like when we realize that we don't have enough time to finish all of our homework, it can be hard to know what to do about them. But usually we can find a solution or a way to help us deal with our problem. When we're not sure about what to do, we can use these **problem-solving steps** to help us choose the best solution.

You'll eventually learn how to do these steps pretty quickly in your head, but it can help to PRACTICE ON PAPER first.

Step 1: What is the problem?

Example: *I don't have enough time to finish my homework.*

Problem: _____

Taking Charge of Worries About Real Things

Step 2: What are some things you could do that would help you deal with the problem?

Solution: *Rush to answer every question, even if it isn't my best job, and hand it in anyways.*

List EVERY idea that comes to mind, not just the ones you think are "good" right now. There are often a lot of different solutions to choose from. You'll learn to think about each solution and choose the one that will work best for you.

Solution 1: _____

Solution 2: _____

Solution 3: _____

Solution 4: _____

Solution 5: _____

Solution 6: _____

Step 3: What are some **pros** (positive things) and **cons** (negative things) about each of your remaining possible solutions? Write down the **pros** and **cons** for each solution in the chart.

	PROS	CONS
Example: *Rush to answer every question, even if it isn't my best job, and hand it in anyways,*	• *I'll finish all the questions and hand my homework in on time.*	• *I'll probably get a lower grade than I usually do.*

	PROS	CONS
Solution 1:		
Solution 2:		
Solution 3:		

	PROS	CONS
Solution 4:		
Solution 5:		
Solution 6:		

Now, cross any solutions that don't meet the following four guidelines, which will help you to find the most helpful solution:

- safe for yourself and others

- fair

- possible in the real world (no genies granting magic wishes!)

- something you can control

Step 4: Look over your completed chart and weigh the pros and cons for each possible solution. Choose the best solution (and keep a backup plan in mind).

Step 5: Try your solution and see if it helps! If it doesn't, try the next best solution until you're happy with the outcome.

Even if your first solution doesn't work out the way you wanted it to, remember that you're learning every time you try to solve a problem. Take your time with this practice, and it will help you to get even better at solving new problems in the future!

Facing Fears: Step-by-Step

When we're worried about doing something that we know is tough for us, or when we're trying something for the first time, we can feel overwhelmed. It can sometimes feel too big and scary to do something hard for us all at once.

It usually helps if we break a difficult task into smaller steps. Let's think this through by reading the **story** of how Jenny became friends with dogs. Notice the steps Jenny takes to face her fear of being around dogs.

Jenny's Step-by-Step Plan

Jenny's best friend Sarah has a new puppy named Ranger. Sarah really wants Jenny to come and meet him. But Jenny has a problem—she is really afraid of dogs! Jenny really wants to meet Ranger because Sarah is so excited about him, and she wants to keep going over to Sarah's house to play, but she doesn't know how to deal with her fear of dogs. She is afraid that even if she tried to go, she would get too nervous and uncomfortable to stay, and then she might feel embarrassed. She would really like to find a way to be comfortable around Ranger, and maybe even help Sarah take him for walks, but she's not sure how.

Jenny's brother suggested going right over to Sarah's house and facing her fear all at once, like "ripping off a bandage." But that felt like way too much right away and she started to feel panicked just imagining it. Jenny's aunt listened to her and helped her break down her goal into smaller steps. She told her it was okay to take her time practicing each step until she felt comfortable. Jenny didn't feel panicked anymore. Whenever she started to worry about it, she reminded herself to take it **"one step at a time."**

First, Jenny's mom took her to the public library so she could take out a **book** about puppies. She found one that was all about how to take care of and train a new puppy. This made Jenny feel like she knew a little more about dogs. Then she watched a movie about dogs, which helped her imagine being around them.

Next, Jenny and her parents went to a **dog park** to watch dogs playing. They watched the dogs playing from outside the fence and didn't go inside. At first, Jenny was really nervous that a dog would somehow come near her. She started to feel hot and shaky, and her heart would beat fast, but her parents helped her practice taking deep belly breaths. This helped Jenny relax. Jenny was surprised to see that so many dogs could get along so well. Sometimes, a dog would take another dog's toy or bother another dog, and sometimes they would bark at one another, but they usually got over it pretty quickly, or the owners would call their dogs away. Jenny repeated this step over and over by going to the dog park every Saturday for several weeks. Her parents would even take her for ice cream on the way home as a reward for Jenny working on reaching her goal.

Jenny eventually felt ready to **get closer** to a dog. There was a small dog named Rolie she had seen at the dog park every week. He had short little legs, which meant he had to wiggle his little feet faster than the other dogs to keep up. This made Jenny smile. This dog also seemed really friendly and gentle. Jenny mentioned to her parents that she thought she might be comfortable around that dog. The owner had even smiled at Jenny one day while Jenny was watching Rolie play.

One day, Jenny saw Rolie approaching the park gate and the owner stopped to say hi. Rolie wiggled his tail and tried to get closer to Jenny. Jenny's parents explained that Jenny was practicing how to feel comfortable around dogs, so Rolie's owner made sure not to let Rolie jump up on Jenny, even though Rolie was really excited. His tail was wagging, and he kept sticking his little tongue out of his mouth. Jenny took a few deep belly breaths and reached out her hand close enough for Rolie to sniff her. Jenny pulled back right away and Rolie just stood there, with a surprised look. Jenny put her hand back out and let Rolie sniff her some more. He even gave her some little licks. Jenny noticed that it tickled a little. On the way home, Jenny was very excited and proud that she had taken that step. Her parents made her favorite meal to celebrate.

After visiting Rolie a few more times, Jenny felt it was time to meet her friend Sarah's puppy. They made a plan for Sarah to hold Ranger on a leash so Jenny could get close as she felt more comfortable. While Jenny got ready to go to Sarah's house, she focused on positive thoughts. *Sarah will be holding the puppy and I only have to get as close as I want. I can breathe to help myself relax,* she reminded herself. This helped her feel better, and when her mind began to imagine Ranger growling or even biting her, she challenged that thought by asking herself, *Has Ranger ever hurt anyone before?* The answer was no. Instead of thinking scary thoughts, Jenny decided to prepare herself by imagining her meeting with Ranger going well. She imagined that Ranger was friendly like Rolie. Jenny also remembered that her parents promised to take her to her favorite restaurant for a meal when she finally reached her goal. She was looking forward to how proud she would feel when she was able to pet Ranger—and she did! She even felt brave enough to let Sarah take off Ranger's leash while they played together on the floor. That evening, Jenny's parents took both her and Sarah to Jenny's favorite restaurant to celebrate!

Now, let's think about the steps that Jenny took to face her fear.

Read each step Jenny took and try to place them in order. Write a number between 1 and 8 next to each step in the order she took, with 1 being the first step she took, and 8 being the last step she took.

_____ *Jenny watched dogs at the dog park.*

_____ *Jenny petted Ranger.*

_____ *Jenny imagined Ranger being friendly with her.*

_____ *Jenny looked at books about dogs and learned more about them.*

_____ *Jenny played on the floor with Ranger.*

_____ *Jenny touched Rolie at the dog park.*

_____ *Jenny watched a movie about dogs and imagined being around them.*

_____ *Jenny decided she would like to meet Rolie.*

Write down some of the positive thoughts that Jenny told herself when she was preparing to meet Ranger.

_____

_____

_____

_____

What question did she ask herself to challenge her negative thoughts when she IMAGINED that Ranger would growl at her or bite her?

_____

_____

Match each reward to the order it happened. Draw a line from each number to the reward Jenny received each time she took a step toward her goal, with 1 being the first reward she got and 4 being the last reward.

4   Jenny got ice cream.

3   Jenny's parents took her and Sarah out for dinner.

2   Jenny felt proud.

1   Jenny's parents made her favorite meal.

Making a Step-by-Step Plan

You can make your own **step-by-step plan** to meet a goal.

1. **Name your final goal!** This can be something new that you want to achieve, or a fear you would like to overcome.

2. **Think of the practice steps** you'll take to work up to your final goal.

3. **List each step in order from easiest to hardest.** List the easiest at the bottom and work your way up.

4. **List who could help you** next to each step.

5. **Write positive thoughts** that could help you next to each step. If you're having trouble moving from negative, scary thoughts to positive, helpful thoughts, use some of the questions you learned to challenge yourself.

6. **Come up with reward ideas** to help you really want to reach each step. Rewards don't have to be things or money—you can do something you find relaxing, or you can do special activities with the important people in your life, such as going to a special place with your best friend or making a special meal with your family. Even the feeling of pride can be a reward on its own! But if there's something really important that you've been wanting to do, this might be a good way to earn it. You (and your family) can come up with the rewards that work for you!

7. **Try the steps.** Start by just focusing on the first step. Remember to use your positive thoughts at each step, ask for help if you need it, and give yourself a reward after each step. You can work on each step as long as you need to before moving on to the next step. After you finish one step, move on to the next, and keep practicing until you reach your goal!

Taking Charge of Worries About Real Things

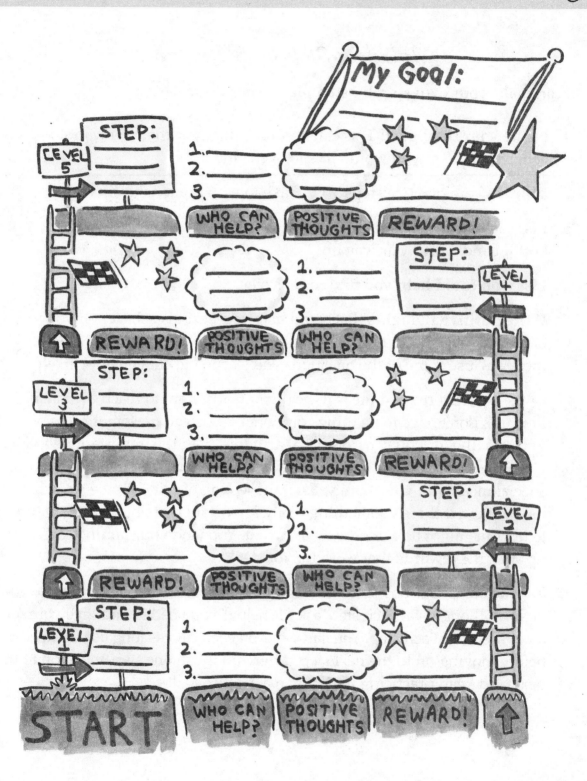

Chapter 6

Taking Charge of
My Imagination

Taking Charge of My Imagination

Sometimes we have worries about real-life things or things that could possibly happen. We've learned to keep ourselves safe, problem solve, and practice taking steps to make scary things feel easier.

Some of the things that we worry about aren't likely to happen, and certainly aren't happening right now, even though it might feel like they are. These things exist **only in our imagination**. Sometimes, the more creative we are, the more scary things we can imagine to worry about.

But, because we have that strong imagination, we can learn to use it to help us— by training our imagination to go in the direction we want it to! Keep reading to learn how!

The Anxiety Workbook for Kids

Taking Charge of
My Imagination

Worry

Sometimes it can feel like worry just keeps picking on us and won't go away! It might bother us by getting us to think of things to be afraid of, or it might keep telling us about all the things that could possibly go wrong. We might even imagine that worry is a nasty character, maybe a monster, that keeps pestering us! But the good news is, we can use our imaginations to help us **stand up to worry** when it's not being helpful.

Imagine what worry might look like and draw it here. It can look like anything you want—a person, a monster, or any type of creature you can think of. You can even name it if you want to!

Worry's Words:

Fill in the word balloons with some of the things worry might say when it's around.

Huebner, D. (2006)]

Standing Up to Worry

What are some things you could say to stand up to worry? Write down some of your ideas in the word balloons. Then, use your imagination to practice standing up to worry when it picks on you.

My Worry Buddy

Now, imagine that you have a buddy to help you when worry is around. Your new friend might give you ideas on how to stand up to worry, or remind you of things that help you feel confident and relaxed.

Imagine what your buddy might look like, and draw it here. It can look like anyone or anything you want! You can even give your new pal a name.

My Worry Buddy's Words

Write some things your worry buddy might say to help you stand up to worry—and feel calm and confident! Your worry buddy might ask if the things worry says are really true, or point out something positive you weren't noticing, or even help solve a problem that's worrying you.

Taking Charge of My Imagination

"Even Though..."

Sometimes, worry can get us to think about lots of bad things that could happen (even if those things are not very likely). Standing up to worry can help us to feel more confident and in control.

A trick that lots of kids find helpful when worry is getting them to think about all the bad things that could happen is to use the comeback **"Even though** _____, **that doesn't mean** _____."

Here are some examples:

- **Even though** we have emergency drills at school, **that doesn't mean** there will be a real emergency today.

- **Even though** my friend is taking a long time to get here, **that doesn't mean** something bad happened to her.

- **Even though** my mom is late picking me up, **that doesn't mean** she will leave me here forever.

Now you try!

Even though math isn't my best subject, **that doesn't mean** _____

_____.

Even though _____, **that doesn't mean**

_____.

Taking a Break from Worry

Now that you've learned to stand up to worry, draw it going away and leaving you alone. Imagine how good it feels to take a break from worry!

Draw the Scary Thing...

We've already talked about what we can do with real worries. For example, we can use our problem-solving steps to decide what to do in difficult situations, and we can use our step-by-step plans to help us take small steps to work toward a bigger goal.

Now, we're going to talk about what we can do when those things that we're worried about aren't even possible or real, or at least aren't very likely to happen, and certainly aren't happening right now—even if they do feel very real because of how strong our imagination is! Sometimes, we imagine these things so clearly that it can feel like we're watching a movie in our mind. We might hear a noise outside of our window at night and we might imagine that a bad guy is trying to break into our house. In fact, we may begin to imagine all the details of what he looks like, and even what the intruder might do once he gets inside. In reality, that noise might just be from the wind knocking a branch against the window.

**Draw a worry you can imagine so clearly
that it feels like a movie in your mind.**

...Now Change It

Let's talk about how we can change that movie playing in our mind. But first, answer this: Who owns your mind (and your imagination)? That's right—you! You can decide to become the director of that movie in your mind! This is where it comes in handy to have a strong imagination. Instead of letting that worry take control of your imagination, stand up to your worry bully and choose for yourself what you would like to imagine.

Think about the movie you just described. Now, change it by adding things, such as people, situations, objects, or even magical powers, that will make you feel safer and more in control.

Draw that scene now, and remember to enjoy using your imagination!

Mastering the Worry

When we are very worried or scared, it can feel like our fears and worries are taking over and becoming the boss of us. But, we can use our knowledge and our imagination to master those fears and worries!

Become the Expert (Get to Know Your Fear)

Usually, the more we know about something, the more comfortable and confident we feel around it. For example, if we're going camping, we can learn about the wildlife in the area. This will make us feel like we would know what to do if we came across an animal. This is also why we have fire drills at school—so that we will know what to do if there's ever a real fire, even though it's unlikely.

But, even though it's helpful to learn about something we're worried about so that we can feel more confident, it's also important to not spend too much time focusing on what we're scared of. For example, if we're worried about the world outside our home, it's not a good idea to spend a lot of time watching scary news stories.

Taking Charge of My Imagination

Dress Up as My Fear

We know that doing research about what we're afraid of can help us feel more comfortable with it. The same is true for dressing up like scary things! Imagine dressing up as a zombie or a monster in an environment where you know you're really safe. You might feel more in control of your fear. Try it! Pretend you're a scary thing and have some fun with it. Be silly! This is your time to play!

Draw My Fear...and Turn It Silly

Often when we think of something that we fear, we imagine it to be terrifying!

When we draw our fear, we get to take control of it. We even have the power to turn it into something silly that will make us laugh! Remember when you drew your fear and then added things to feel safer and more in control? Now, draw your fear again, but this time, make it look silly or funny.

Taking Charge of My Imagination

How I've Changed

Now that you've learned all about fears and worries and practiced lots of different ways to take charge of them, let's really think about how far you've come.

Close your eyes and think about how you felt about fears and worries before you started this workbook.

Draw a picture of yourself back then.

Taking Charge of My Worries

Now, close your eyes again and think of how much new knowledge you have inside you, and about all the practice you've done!

Draw a picture of yourself now.

Sharing My Success

We're always changing and learning new things. After a lot of practice, we can become more confident in a lot of new ways!

Tell someone you trust about the things you've learned and some ways that you've become more confident.

To help you think about what you would like to say, you can write about some of the things you've learned here.

When you're done sharing, celebrate your success together!

Chapter 7

Remembering and Staying Motivated

Remembering and Staying Motivated

Worry Scale

Let's learn how to use a scale to measure how worried we are. Try noticing how worried you are before and after practicing with the tools and strategies in this book.

If you're very worried, your worry level might be a 10, at the top of the scale. If you're only a little worried, you might be a 4 or a 5.

After you figure out what your worry level is, try one of the strategies you've learned in this book. Then notice if your worry level has gone down. **Measuring your worry level before and after** using a strategy will help you find out which ideas are most helpful to you.

You can use this scale to measure your worry level at any time.

The Anxiety Workbook for Kids

Make It a Competition

Sometimes, a little competition can encourage us. Imagine that there are two teams in this competition: your team and the worry team. The worry team scores a point if they can get a worry into your net and make it stick! But, if you're able to use any of the skills or strategies you practiced to make that worry smaller or less scary, then your team gets the point instead! You can use your worry scale to help you figure out if your worry got any smaller. If it did, you get a point!

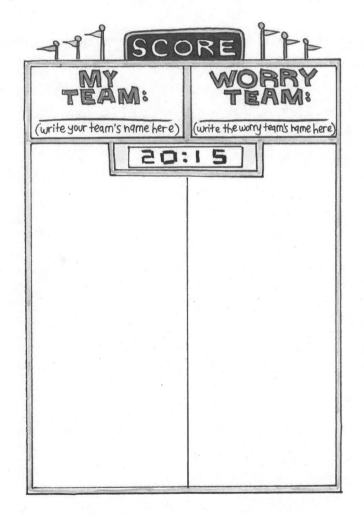

Remember to reward yourself!

Remembering and Staying Motivated

Remember

You've done a lot of hard work! Try to keep everything you've learned about yourself and how to take charge of fears and worries fresh in your mind.

Review this book from time to time, and notice if anything changes for you.

Also, a great way to really understand something is to think of how you would explain it to someone else.

Imagine that a friend with fears and worries asks you about this book. They want to know what it's about and how it can be helpful. What would you tell them?

Write what you would say below.

My Very Own Worry Plan Poster

Make a poster of the strategies that you find most helpful.

You can go to http://www.newharbinger.com/34770 and print out words and pictures from this book to cut out and use in your poster. (Ask a parent for help if you need to.) You'll find words and pictures that can remind you to:

remember your body clues

or

practice thinking positive thoughts

or

choose a solution and try it out

or

visit your peaceful place

or

draw your fear and make it silly

or

become the director of your own imagination

**or any other idea or inspiration that you want to
remember and use!**

Draw or write in anything else you want to add to your poster. Decorate it however you like!

Post it somewhere you will see it often so it can be a daily reminder for you!

Robin Alter, PhD, CPsych, received her undergraduate degree from Skidmore College in Saratoga Springs, NY, and her master's and doctoral degrees from the University of Florida in Gainesville, FL. She was the head of the children's program at Tri-County Mental Health in Northern Florida before moving to Toronto, ON, Canada, where she has been working in children's mental health in since 1980. Alter has been employed by two of the largest children's mental health centers in the Toronto area for over thirty-six years—The Hincks-Dellcrest Centre, and Blue Hills Child and Family Centre.

Alter also works with Anishnawbe Health Toronto, providing fetal alcohol assessments for the people of the First Nations community. She has taught psychology at York University, and maintains a private practice with Alter, Stuckler and Associates in the Toronto area. She is a trustee with the Psychology Foundation of Canada. Alter gives many public lectures to parent groups, teachers, and principals, and has been on numerous radio and television programs talking about children's mental health issues. She is author of *Anxiety and the Gift of Imagination*, and is the anxiety expert for the website, the ABCs of Mental Health.

Crystal Clarke, MSW, RSW, received her undergraduate social work degree from Memorial University of Newfoundland in Canada in 2007. Before continuing on to complete her master's degree, Clarke worked as a social worker with Child, Youth and Family Services in the city of St. John's, NL, Canada, while also supporting foster families through her involvement on the board of the Newfoundland and Labrador Foster Families Association. Clarke received her master's of social work degree at the University of Toronto in 2010, where she specialized in clinical practice with children and families, and also completed a collaborative program in addiction studies. By 2009, Clarke was involved with The Hincks-Dellcrest Centre, one of the largest children's mental health centers in Toronto, ON, Canada, where she was employed as a child and family therapist until 2016, when she decided to leave that position in order to support children and youth within the school system in Toronto.

Additionally, Clarke maintains her own private practice, Clarke Psychotherapy, in Toronto. In 2015, Clarke was also appointed as an adjunct lecturer for the Factor-Inwentash Faculty of Social Work at the University of Toronto as a result of her ongoing commitment to the training and supervision of social work students. Clarke continues to expand upon her own knowledge and expertise in the field of mental health through her training as a psychoanalytic candidate at the Toronto Institute for Contemporary Psychoanalysis.

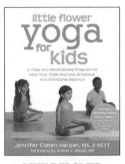
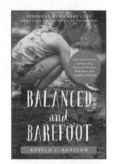

Register your **new harbinger** titles for additional benefits!

When you register your **new harbinger** title—purchased in any format, from any source—you get access to benefits like the following:

- Downloadable accessories like printable worksheets and extra content
- Instructional videos and audio files
- Information about updates, corrections, and new editions

Not every title has accessories, but we're adding new material all the time.

Access free accessories in 3 easy steps:

1. Sign in at NewHarbinger.com (or **register** to create an account).

2. Click on **register a book**. Search for your title and click the **register** button when it appears.

3. Click on the **book cover or title** to go to its details page. Click on **accessories** to view and access files.

That's all there is to it!

If you need help, visit:

NewHarbinger.com/accessories